Fiona Goble's
Farmyard Knits

Fiona Goble's
Farmyard Knits

Ivy Press

First published in the UK in 2012 by
Ivy Press
210 High Street
Lewes
East Sussex BN7 2NS
United Kingdom
www.ivypress.co.uk

British Library Cataloguing-in-Publication Data
A catalogue record for this book is available from the British Library

ISBN: 978-1-908005-43-4

This book was conceived, designed and produced by
Ivy Press
Creative Director *Peter Bridgewater*
Publisher *Sophie Collins*
Editorial Director *Tom Kitch*
Senior Designer *James Lawrence*
Designer *Kathryn Gammon*
Photographer *Andrew Perris*
Illustrator *Sarah Goodreau*

Printed in China

Colour origination by Ivy Press Reprographics

10 9 8 7 6 5 4 3 2 1

Contents

Introduction

Most small children love to visit a working farm. This touching and amusing look at a day in the (knitted) farming life comes in woolly form, introducing a full cast of characters, from Anna and Frank, who hold the show together, to Bess the collie, who runs rings around the sheep.

Sweet storybook pages pinpointing special moments in the working day are interleaved with simple instructions for knitting the whole farm, from cows and sheep to pigs and hens – and not forgetting the farm's horse, a fabulously squidgy woollen tractor and a play mat that can serve as anything from an action play setting during the day to a comfort blanket at night.

All of the characters can be made with basic knitting skills, and you'll find that, once you've begun, you'll want to complete the whole line-up, creating a set that will offer years of traditional and refreshingly wholesome play.

Before you begin

There's nothing worse than getting the urge to knit, gathering all your yarn together, and then realizing that you're missing something vital. Or worse still, that yarn you thought was perfect turns out to be not quite right. So to avoid frustration and disappointment, check through your craft box before you begin. And if you need to, write yourself a knitted farmyard shopping list.

Knitting needles & crochet hooks

Knitting needles

These are available in many different materials, including wood, plastic and various metals. The choice is up to you.

You will need a pair of knitting needles in each of the following sizes:

◊ Size 2.25 mm (US 1)
◊ Size 2.75 mm (US 2)
◊ Size 3 mm (US 2 or 3)
◊ Size 3.25 mm (US 3)

The main parts of most of the projects are knitted on size 3 mm (US 2 or 3) needles.

Because the projects are small, if you are buying new knitting needles we recommend that you buy the shortest-length needles, which are usually 23 cm (9 in). It is also helpful to have needles with quite sharply pointed ends, because the project pieces are knitted quite tightly and sharply pointed needles make it easier to get into the stitches.

Crochet hook

While there is hardly any crochet in these projects, for some of the items you will need to know how to crochet a simple chain and work a simple crochet edge (see page 16).

Choose size 3.25 mm (US D-3) and size 4.25 mm (US G-6) hooks, if you are buying them specially. However, If you already have hooks within a size or two of these, they will do the job perfectly well.

Sewing needles

A needle to sew your knitted pieces together

You will need a needle with a fairly blunt end and an eye large enough for threading yarn to sew your projects together. These are sometimes sold as 'yarn needles', but an ordinary tapestry needle will also work well.

An embroidery needle

You will need an embroidery needle, which has a sharper end than a yarn or tapestry needle, to embroider the finishing touches on your projects. Make sure that the eye of the needle is large enough for you to thread your yarn through it.

An ordinary sewing needle

You will need an ordinary sewing needle to sew on buttons and a few other finishing touches.

Other tools

A stitch holder, large safety pin or spare knitting needle

In some of the projects, you will need to keep some of your knitting stitches safe while you work on another part of the project. You can use a special stitch holder for this. Alternatively, you can use a spare knitting needle or large safety pin.

Some small safety pins

You will need these to mark the beginning and end of certain rows in some of the projects.

Some small sharp scissors

You will need these to cut your yarn and trim all your yarn tails.

A tape measure or ruler

You will need this to check your tension and, in some projects, for measuring your knitting.

A water-soluble pen

This is a special type of felt pen that you can use on fabric or yarn that you can later spray or wipe away with water. They are very useful for marking the position of the features on dolls and animals before you embroider them. They are widely available in craft, sewing and haberdashery shops.

A red colouring pencil

You will need an ordinary red colouring pencil (not a wax crayon or felt pen) to rub over your finished knitted farmer and his wife to make their cheeks look nice and rosy.

A small nylon brush

You will need a small nylon brush to fluff up the yarn on some of your finished animals. A nail brush or tooth brush with nylon bristles should work fine.

Materials

Knitting yarns

Almost all the projects are knitted in standard double knitting yarn. It does not matter what brand you choose and you can mix brands within your project. You may also want to choose different colours than the ones we have used. However, it is very important to choose yarns that are 100 per cent wool or acrylic/wool mixes. Cotton yarns or 100 per cent acrylic yarns – particularly cheaper acrylic yarns – will lead to disappointing results.

Some of the projects also require small amounts of specialist yarns, such as mohair.

Polyester stuffing

All the projects are stuffed with 100 per cent polyester toy stuffing. This is a light, fluffy white mixture specially manufactured for craft items. It is widely available in craft and haberdashery shops. Always check that the stuffing you are using conforms to safety standards.

Foam board

You will need some foam board (sometimes called foam core) for the tractor base to keep it rigid. Foam board consists of a layer of Styrofoam, coated on both sides with paper. It is lightweight and rigid. Foam board is available in most art and craft shops.

Ordinary sewing thread

For a few of the projects you will need some standard polyester sewing thread.

Tension

The knitting tension for the patterns in this book is 12 sts and 16 rows to 4 cm ($1^1/_2$ in) square over st st on 3 mm (US 2/3) needles.

When knitting small items like the ones in this book, your knitting tension is not as vital as when you are knitting clothes. The main thing is to make sure that your knitted fabric is firm enough for your items to keep their shape and for the stuffing not to show through. If you knit unusually tightly, however, you may want to use slightly larger needles than those recommended. If you knit particularly loosely, choose slightly smaller knitting needles.

Abbreviations

The following abbreviations are used in the knitting patterns in this book.

K	knit
P	purl
st(s)	stitch(es)
st st	stocking stitch
beg	beginning
k2tog	knit the next 2 stitches together
p2tog	purl the next 2 stitches together
p3tog	purl the next 3 stitches together
kwise	by knitting the stitch or stitches
pwise	by purling the stitch or stitches
inc1	increase one stitch by knitting into the front and then the back of the next stitch
loop1	make a loop stitch (see page 14)
M1	make one stitch by picking up the horizontal loop before the next stitch and knitting into the back of it
s1	slip one (slip a stitch onto the right-hand needle without knitting it)
psso	pass slipped stitch over (pass the slipped stitch over the stitch just knitted)
ssk	slip, slip, knit (slip 2 stitches, one at a time, then knit the slipped stitches together)
yf	yarn forward (bring the yarn from the back of the work to the front)
LH	left-hand
RH	right-hand
RS	right side

WS	wrong side
mb	make a bobble (see page 14)
rem	remaining
rep	repeat
f	front
b	back
g	gram
oz	ounce
mm	millimetre
cm	centimetre
in	inch
m	metre
yd	yard

Brackets, parentheses & asterisks

Sometimes you will need to repeat an instruction once or more within a row of knitting. In this case, the instruction is given in square brackets and the number of times you need to repeat the instruction is given just outside. For example, [k2tog] 3 times means you need to knit two stitches together three times.

The figures given at the end of rows in parentheses (round brackets) indicate the number of stitches you should have on your needle once you have completed that row.

An asterisk (*) marks where a section should be repeated in another part of the pattern.

Knitting guide

Most of the projects in this book are very straightforward and you do not need to know any complicated techniques. So if you are familiar with casting on and casting off, both knitwise and purlwise, and if you can knit and purl, increase and decrease – then you know practically all you need. Knitting every row is known as garter stitch, alternating rows of knit and purl stitches is called stocking stitch and alternating knit and purl stitches to make columns is called ribbing.

Casting on

We recommend the cable casting-on method, for which you will need to use both your knitting needles.

1 Make a slip knot in your yarn leaving a long yarn tail (about 25 cm/10 in), which you can use later for sewing your finished item together. To make the knot, arrange your yarn in a loop. Using your needle, pull a loop of yarn through this loop and keep it on your needle. Pull the knot up quite tightly. This slip knot forms your first cast-on stitch.

2 Holding the needle with the slip knot in your left hand, insert the point of your RH needle into the slip knot and under the LH needle. Wind the yarn around the tip of the RH needle.

3 Draw the yarn through the slip knot with the point of your RH needle to form a loop.

4 Transfer the loop from the RH to the LH needle to form the second stitch.

5 To make the next stitch, insert your RH needle between the two stitches on the LH needle. Wind the yarn over the RH needle from left to right.

6 With your RH needle, pull the yarn through the gap to form a loop in a similar way to the action in step 3. Transfer this loop to your LH needle to form your third stitch.

Repeat steps 5 and 6 until you have the number of stitches you need.

The knit stitch

This is the basic knitting stitch.

1 Holding the needle with your cast-on stitches in your left hand, poke the tip of your RH needle into the front of the first cast-on stitch from left to right.

2 Wind your yarn around the tip of your RH needle from the left side to the right side.

3 Pull the yarn through the original stitch to form a loop on your RH needle. This loop will be your new stitch.

4 Slip the original stitch off your LH needle. Your new stitch will now be on your RH needle.

Repeat these steps until you have knitted all your stitches. To work the next row, hold the needle with your knitting stitches in your left hand.

The purl stitch

This is like working a knit stitch backwards and is the second basic knitting stitch.

1 Holding the needle with your knitted stitches in your left hand, poke the tip of your RH needle through the front of the first stitch from right to left.

2 Wind your yarn around the needle from right to left.

3 With the tip of your RH needle, pull the yarn through the original stitch to form a loop. This loop will be your new stitch.

4 Slip the original stitch off the LH needle. Your new stitch will now be on your RH needle.

Repeat these steps until you have purled all your stitches. To work the next row, hold the needle with your knitting stitches in your left hand.

Casting off

When you have finished your knitting, you will need to cast off to prevent your work from unravelling. You will need to do this knitwise or purlwise depending on the pattern.

Casting off knitwise

1 Knit two stitches in the normal way. Using the tip of your LH needle, pick up the first stitch you knitted and lift it over the second stitch.

2 You have now cast off the first stitch. Now knit another stitch so that you have two stitches on your needle again.

Repeat steps 1 and 2 until you have only one stitch left on your RH needle. Cut the yarn, leaving a long yarn tail (about 25 cm/10 in). Pull the yarn tail through the last stitch you have knitted.

Casting off purlwise

This is just like casting off knitwise, except that you purl instead of knit all the stitches.

1 Purl two stitches in the normal way. Using the tip of your LH needle, pick up the first stitch you knitted and lift it over the second stitch.

2 You have now cast off the first stitch. Now purl another stitch so that you have two stitches on your needle again.

Repeat steps 1 and 2 until you have only one stitch left on your RH needle. Cut the yarn, leaving a long yarn tail (about 25 cm/10 in). Pull the yarn tail through the last stitch you have knitted.

Increasing stitches

There are two main ways to increase the number of stitches on your needle. The method you use depends on where you need to create the new stitch.

Increasing m1

This involves making an additional stitch between two existing stitches.

1 Pick up the horizontal strand that runs between the stitch you have just knitted and the next one, using the tip of your RH needle.

2 Transfer the strand to your LH needle to form a loop by inserting your LH needle through the strand from right to left.

3 To complete, knit through the back of the stitch.

Occasionally, you will need to make a stitch in a purl row. This is done in the same way only you purl through the back of the stitch rather than knit.

Increasing inc1

This involves making an additional stitch at the same time as knitting the next stitch.

Start by knitting your stitch in the normal way, but instead of slipping the original stitch straight off your needle, knit through the back of it to create an additional stitch. Then slip the original stitch off your needle in the normal way.

Decreasing stitches

Your choice of decrease stitch depends on how many stitches you need to decrease and where the decrease is needed.

Decreasing k2tog

Poke your RH needle from left to right through two stitches instead of the normal one and knit in the normal way.

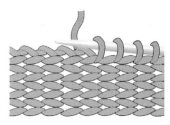

Decreasing p2tog

Poke your RH needle from right to left through two stitches instead of the normal one and purl in the normal way.

In one of the projects, you will also need to p3tog. This is done in exactly the same as p2tog, except that you poke your needle through three stitches instead of two.

Decreasing ssk

Slip the first stitch from your LH to your RH needle without knitting it. Slip the next stitch in the same way.

Then insert the tip of your LH needle through the front loops of both the slipped stitches and knit them in the normal way.

Decreasing s1, k2tog, psso

This is a method to decrease two stitches at a time.

1 Slip the first stitch from your LH to your RH needle without knitting it. Knit the next two stitches together.

2 Use the tip of your LH needle to lift the slipped stitch over the stitch in front of it and off the needle.

Picking up stitches along an edge

For some of the projects, you will need to pick up and knit stitches along a finished vertical edge (the edges of your rows) or horizontal edge (a cast-on or cast-off edge).

Vertical edge

With the right side of your work facing you, insert the tip of your needle between the first stitches of the first two rows.

Wind your yarn around the needle and pull the loop through. Wind your yarn around your needle again and pull the stitch through to form the first picked-up and knitted stitch.

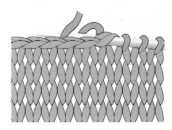

You will normally find that you have more gaps between rows than stitches you need to pick up and knit. To make sure your work is even, you will have to miss a gap between rows every few rows.

Horizontal edge

This is worked in the same way as picking up stitches along a vertical edge, except that you work through the cast-on or cast-off stitches rather than the gaps between rows.

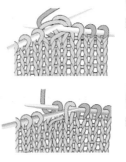

Fancy stitches

Making a bobble

For the cabbage patch in the play mat, you will need to know how to make a bobble.

1 On the right side of your work, [K1, P1] twice into the next stitch and slip all the stitches onto your RH needle. Turn your work and purl 4 stitches. Turn your work again and knit 4 stitches. Turn your work again and purl 4 stitches.

2 Turn your work so that the RS is facing. Slip the first 2 stitches onto your RH needle. Then knit 2 stitches together. Pass the two slipped sts over the other stitch.

Loop stitch

For the farm dog, you will also need to know how to work loop stitch.

1 Knit a stitch in the normal way, but do not pull the original stitch off your needle. Bring your yarn from the back to the front of your work between your needles. Loop the yarn around your thumb.

2 Take the yarn back between the needles and knit the stitch from the LH needle in the normal way.

3 Pass the stitch on the right over the stitch on the left to secure the loop.

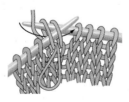

A good old stitch-up

Once you have knitted all the pieces for your project, you will need to stitch them together. The joining methods you will need to use are specified in the making-up instructions for each project.

Mattress stitch

There are two versions of this stitch – one to join vertical edges such as the main seams on the farmer's arms and the other to join horizontal edges such as the lower edges of the farmer's body.

Vertical edges

Place the two edges side by side, with the RS of your work facing you. Take your needle under the running thread between the first two stitches of one side, then under the corresponding running thread of the other side.

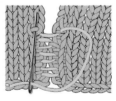

Pull your yarn up fairly tightly (but not so tightly that your work puckers) every few stitches.

Horizontal edges

Place the two edges side by side, with the RS of your work facing you. Take your needle under the two 'legs' of the last row of stitches on the first piece of knitting.

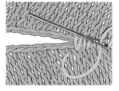

Then take your needle under the two 'legs' of the corresponding stitch on the second piece of knitting.

Alternative to oversewing

Instead of oversewing (see page 15), you can use this stitch to join smaller parts such as limbs to bigger parts such as bodies.

Oversewing

This stitch is used to join small pieces of work and pieces that have curved edges. It is normally worked with the pieces RS together.

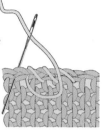

The stitch is worked by taking the yarn from the front of your work, over the edge of the seam and out through the front again a short distance further on.

A version of oversewing is also used to join very small pieces of knitting, such as the ears, to the main part of the doll or animal.

Creating a flat seam

When you join the play mat sections together, you will need to create a completely flat seam. To do this, first lay the two pieces to be joined RS up and next to each other. Using your yarn needle, pick up the very outermost strand of knitting from one side and then the other, working your way along the seam and pulling your yarn up firmly every few stitches. The technique is almost identical whether you are joining two vertical or two horizontal edges.

Seams worked like this are not quite as invisible as mattress stitch but, unlike mattress stitch, your pieces will lie completely flat.

Other joining techniques

For some of the projects you will also need to know how to work a simple running stitch and a simple back stitch.

Running stitch

To work running stitch, simply take your needle in and out of your work, keeping the stitch length and the gaps between stitches even.

Back stitch

To work back stitch, first bring your needle out at your starting point.

Work a single running stitch, taking your needle out of your work a stitch width in front of the first stitch.

Now take your needle back into your work at the end point of the first stitch and out again a stitch width in front of the end of the second stitch.

Continue in this way until your stitching is complete.

Weaving in the yarn tail ends

When sewing the dolls or animals themselves, the yarn tails can be concealed simply within the main body of the animal.

When you have finished sewing the item together, take the needle into the item and bring it out at another point.

Pull the yarn tail firmly and squash your item slightly. Trim the yarn tail so that when your item springs back into shape, the yarn tail end will be concealed inside.

In the case of small pieces such as the tips of some of the animals' ears, you may need to run your yarn tail down the side of a piece and into the main part of the body.

On items such as the farmer's and farmer's wife's clothes, conceal the yarn tail ends in the seam by working a few oversewing stitches forwards then backwards and then trimming the yarn tail close to your work.

Taking your needle between the strands that make up the yarn rather than between stitches will help make sure the yarn tail stays in place.

Shaping your pieces

Some of the pieces that are not stuffed – for example, the play mat and the clothes for the farmer and his wife – will need some final shaping after they have been knitted and made up.

Soak the item in plain warm water, gently wring it out and pull it into shape.

Keep the item flat and let it dry thoroughly.

A touch of crochet & embroidery

The projects only involve a little crochet, but you will need to know how to make a simple crochet chain for some of animals and, for the play mat, you will need to know how to work a simple crochet edging. You will also need to know a few basic embroidery stitches to embroider the features on your toys and animals and to embroider the flowers on the play mat.

Crochet chain

1 Make a slip knot on the crochet hook as if you were starting to cast on some knitting. Holding the slip stitch on the hook, wind the yarn around the hook from the back to the front. Then catch the yarn in the crochet hook tip.

2 Pull the yarn through the slip stitch on your crochet hook to make the second link in the chain. Continue in this way until the chain is the length that you need.

Crochet edging

1 To work crochet edging along a vertical edge, insert your crochet hook between the first stitches of the first two rows from front to back. Wind your yarn round your crochet hook and pull a loop of yarn through. Wind your yarn around the hook and draw it through the loop.

2 Insert the hook two stitches along, draw a loop through, wind the yarn round the hook and draw it through the two loops on the hook.

Take care to make sure that the edging is firm – but not so tight that it 'gathers' the fabric or so loose that it makes the edges 'frill'.

Crochet edging along a horizontal edge is worked in exactly the same way, except that you insert your hook into the spaces between stitches rather than into the spaces between the edges of your rows.

Satin stitch

This stitch is used for the cat's nose. It consists of a series of straight stitches worked very closely together.

Take your needle out at your starting point. Insert your needle back into your work and out again near the starting point, ready to work the next stitch. Continue in this way until the shape is filled.

> Remember that when embroidering on knitting, it is better to take your needle in and out of your work between the strands that make up your yarn rather than between the stitches themselves. This will help make your embroidery look firmer and more even.

French knots

This stitch is used for the centres of the eyes and for the flower centres on the play mat.

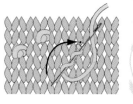

Bring your needle and yarn out at your starting point on the front of your work. Wind the yarn two or three times around the needle and take it back into your work, just to the side of your starting point.

Bring your needle out at the starting point for the next French knot or, if you are working the last knot, at an inconspicuous point on your item.

Continue pulling your needle through your work and slide the knot off the needle and onto your knitted fabric.

Chain stitch

This stitch is used for the whites around the eyes.

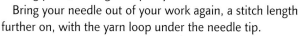

Bring your needle and yarn out at the starting point on the front of your work.

Take your needle back into your knitted fabric just next to your starting point, leaving a loop of yarn.

Bring your needle out of your work again, a stitch length further on, with the yarn loop under the needle tip.

Pull your yarn up firmly, but without pulling your knitting.

Straight stitch

This stitch is used for the dolls' mouths and some of the animals' mouths.

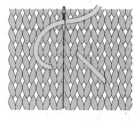

Bring your needle and yarn out at your starting point and take it back down into your work where you want the stitch to end.

For some of the mouths, you will need to make two or three straight stitches in a V or Y shape.

Lazy daisy stitch

This stitch is used for the flower petals on the play mat.

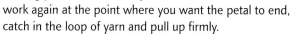

Bring your needle and yarn out at your starting point at the centre of the flower.

Take your needle back into your knitted fabric just next to your starting point, leaving a loop of yarn.

Bring your needle out of your work again at the point where you want the petal to end, catch in the loop of yarn and pull up firmly.

Now take your needle over the edge of the loop of yarn to secure it and back to the centre, ready to work your next petal. Continue in this way until the flower is complete.

Daybreak: collecting the eggs

Frank and Anna are farmers. Through the year, they work with their animals, sow and harvest their crops, and spend all day out of doors. It's barely light, but Anna's already out collecting the eggs. Like everyone else on the farm, the hens have been busy. It's a nice, quiet job to do first thing in the morning, and when Anna has put the day's eggs into a basket, she goes back to the farmhouse to make some coffee.

Frank

Up at daybreak and there's a mountain of work to get done. The cows need milking, the sheep need herding . . . never mind feeding Bess and Max. A farmer's life isn't easy. However, if you love animals and the open air and if, like Frank, you prefer your clothes practical rather than stylish, it could be the life for you.

You will need

15 g/½ oz (37 m/40½ yd) cream DK yarn

2 g/¹⁄₁₆ oz (5 m/5½ yd) white DK yarn

7.5 g/¼ oz (18 m/20 yd) yellow DK yarn

9.5 g/³⁄₈ oz (23 m/25 yd) denim blue DK yarn

4.5 g/⅛ oz (11 m/12 yd) grey DK yarn

4 g/⅛ oz (10 m/11 yd) dark olive green DK yarn

Very small amounts of mid-green, dark brown, black and dark red DK yarns

20 g/¾ oz polyester toy filling

Size 3 mm (US 2/3) knitting needles

Size 2.75 mm (US 2) knitting needles

Size 3.25 mm (US D-3) crochet hook

A yarn needle to sew your work together

An embroidery needle

A red colouring pencil for colouring the cheeks

Doll

Head

The head pieces are knitted from the chin up to the forehead.

Back
Make 1
◊ Using size 3 mm (US 2/3) needles, cast on 13 sts in cream.
◊ First row: Inc1, K to last 2 sts, inc1, K1. (15 sts)
◊ Next row: P.
◊ Next row: K2, M1, K to last 2 sts, M1, K2. (17 sts)*
◊ Work 15 rows in st st, beg with a P row.
◊ Next row: K2, k2tog, K to last 4 sts, ssk, K2. (15 sts)
◊ Next row: P2tog, P to last 2 sts, p2tog. (13 sts)
◊ Rep last 2 rows once more. (9 sts)
◊ Cast off.

Front
Make 1
◊ Work as for front as far as *.
◊ Work 7 rows in st st, beg with a K row.
◊ Next row: K8, K into f and b of next st, turn work, P2, turn work again, K to end. (18 sts)
◊ Next row: P8, p2tog, P8. (17 sts)
◊ Work 6 rows in st st, beg with a K row.

◊ Next row: K2, k2tog, K to last 4 sts, ssk, K2. (15 sts)
◊ Next row: P2tog, P to last 2 sts, p2tog. (13 sts)
◊ Rep last 2 rows once more. (9 sts)
◊ Cast off.

Ears

Make 2
◊ Using size 3 mm (US 2/3) needles, cast on 4 sts in cream.
◊ First row: [K2tog] twice. (2 sts)
◊ Next row: P2tog. (1 st)
◊ Break yarn and pull it through rem st.

Body

The body is knitted from the lower edge to the neck edge.

Make 2 pieces
◊ Using size 3 mm (US 2/3) needles, cast on 16 sts in white.
◊ Work 8 rows in st st, beg with a K row.
◊ Break white yarn and join yellow yarn.
◊ K 4 rows.
◊ Work 12 rows in st st, beg with a K row.
◊ Next row: Cast off 1 st, K to end. (15 sts)
◊ Next row: Cast off 1 st pwise, P to end. (14 sts)
◊ Cast off.

Legs & feet

The legs and feet are knitted as one piece, from the sole of the foot to the top of the thigh.

Make 2
◊ Using size 3 mm (US 2/3) needles, cast on 26 sts in cream.
◊ Work 4 rows in st st, beg with a K row.
◊ Next row: K6, cast off 14 sts, K to end. (12 sts)
◊ Work 25 rows in st st, beg with a P row.
◊ Cast off.

Arms

The arms are knitted from the top of the shoulder to the tip of the hand.

Make 2
◊ Using size 3 mm (US 2/3) needles, cast on 9 sts in cream.
◊ Work 22 rows in st st, beg with a K row.
◊ Next row: K4, inc1, turn work, P2, turn work again, K to end. (10 sts)
◊ Next row: P4, p2tog, P4. (9 sts)
◊ Next row: K.
◊ Next row: P.
◊ Next row: K2, k2tog, K1, ssk, K2. (7 sts)
◊ Next row: P2tog, P3, p2tog. (5 sts)
◊ Cast off.

Making up

With the head pieces RS together, oversew around the sides and chin. Turn the head RS out through the top and stuff. Seam the top of the head, using mattress stitch.

Working from the lower edge of the body pieces, join one of the side seams, the top seam then the other side seam using mattress stitch. Stuff the body, then close the lower edge using mattress stitch.

With the leg and foot piece RS together, oversew the lower, back and top seams of the foot. Turn the piece RS out and sew the back leg seam, using mattress stitch. Stuff carefully. Complete the second leg in the same way.

With the arm piece RS together, oversew around the hand. Turn the arm RS out and sew the main seam using mattress stitch. Complete the second arm in the same way. Do not stuff the arms.

Join the arms to the top edges of the main body and the legs to the outer edges of the lower body, using mattress stitch. Using the same technique, fasten the head to the body at the back and just under the chin. The face should overlap the top part of the body by about 1 cm (³/₈ in). Oversew the ears in place.

Using black yarn, embroider two French knots for the eyes. Using white yarn, work a ring of chain stitch round each French knot. Using dark red yarn, work two straight stitches, one above the other, for the mouth. Use the red pencil to colour the cheeks.

Using dark brown yarn, work 3 rows of chain stitch across the top of the head for the hair.

Pullover sleeves

The main part of the pullover is knitted as part of the doll, so you only need to knit the sleeves.

Make 2
◊ Using size 3 mm (US 2/3) needles, cast on 12 sts in yellow.
◊ Work 18 rows in st st, beg with a K row.
◊ Cast off.

Making up

Fold the sleeves WS together and sew the side seams, using mattress stitch.

Oversew the top of the sleeves around the very top of the arms and, if you like, roll the sleeves up the arms slightly.

Dungarees

The dungarees are knitted as one piece, apart from the straps, from trouser legs to top.

Make 1
◊ Using size 3 mm (US 2/3) needles, cast on 15 sts in denim blue.
◊ Work 3 rows in st st, beg with a P row.
◊ Next row: P.
◊ Work 19 rows in st st, beg with a P row.*
◊ Break yarn and leave sts on a spare needle or stitch holder.

◊ Work second trouser leg as for first as far as *.
◊ Next row: K 15 sts from second trouser leg, then K 15 sts from first trouser leg. (30 sts)
◊ Work 9 rows in st st, beg with a P row.
◊ K 3 rows.
◊ Next row: Cast off 10 sts, K9 (10 sts on RH needle), cast off 10 sts. (10 sts)
◊ Break yarn and pull it through rem st.
◊ Rejoin yarn to RS of work.
◊ Next row: K.
◊ Next row: K2, P6, K2.
◊ Rep last 2 rows 3 times more.
◊ K 2 rows.
◊ Cast off pwise.

Straps

Make 2
◊ Using size 2.75 mm (US 2) needles, cast on 24 sts in denim blue.
◊ K 1 row.
◊ Cast off.

Making up

Using mattress stitch, join the back seam of the trouser part of the dungarees so that the lowest part of the seam is level with the crotch.

Join the two inside leg seams, again using mattress stitch.

Weave in and trim all the loose yarn tails.

Join the straps at the back waistband and front bib so that they cross over at the back.

Hat

Make 1
◊ Using size 3 mm (US 2/3) needles, cast on 30 sts in grey.
◊ Work 4 rows in st st, beg with a K row.
◊ Next row: Cast off 12 sts, K5 (6 sts on RH needle), cast off 12 sts. (6 sts)
◊ Break yarn and, with WS facing, join yarn to rem 6 sts.
◊ Next row: P.
◊ Next row: K1, M1, K to last st, M1, K1. (8 sts)
◊ Next row: P.
◊ Rep last 2 rows once more. (10 sts)
◊ Work 2 rows in st st, beg with a K row.
◊ Next row: K1, k2tog, K4, ssk, K1. (8 sts)
◊ Next row: P.
◊ Next row: K1, k2tog, K2, ssk, K1. (6 sts)
◊ Cast off pwise.

◊ With RS of top part of hat facing you, pick up and K 30 sts along cast-on edge.
◊ Next row: P.
◊ Next row: K1, [inc1] 28 times, K1. (58 sts)
◊ Work 2 rows in st st, beg with a P row.
◊ Next row: K.
◊ Cast off pwise.

Hatband

Make 1
◊ Using a size 3.25 mm (US D-3) crochet hook, crochet a 12-cm (4¾-in) crochet chain in mid-green yarn.

Making up

Join the back seam of the hat and oversew the top part of the hat to the side band.

Make the hatband into a circle and place over the hat.

Boots

Make 2
◊ Using size 3 mm (US 2/3) needles, cast on 28 sts in dark olive green.
◊ K 2 rows.
◊ Work 4 rows in st st, beg with a K row.
◊ Next row: K7, cast off 14 sts, K to end. (14 sts)
◊ Work 5 rows in st st, beg with a P row.
◊ Next row: K.
◊ Cast off loosely.

Making up

Fold the pieces widthways, RS together.

Oversew the back, lower and upper seams, then turn the boot RS out.

Anna

Anna's work is never done. When she isn't working out on the farm itself, she's making some of her delicious pickles to sell at the farmers' market. To cope with life's demands, Anna is sporting a practical pair of wellies and a 'denim' pinafore. What more could a girl want?

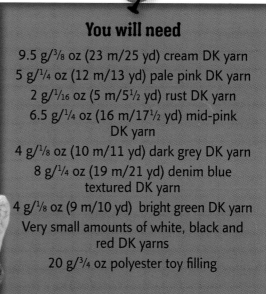

You will need

9.5 g/³⁄₈ oz (23 m/25 yd) cream DK yarn
5 g/¼ oz (12 m/13 yd) pale pink DK yarn
2 g/¹⁄₁₆ oz (5 m/5½ yd) rust DK yarn
6.5 g/¼ oz (16 m/17½ yd) mid-pink DK yarn
4 g/⅛ oz (10 m/11 yd) dark grey DK yarn
8 g/¼ oz (19 m/21 yd) denim blue textured DK yarn
4 g/⅛ oz (9 m/10 yd) bright green DK yarn
Very small amounts of white, black and red DK yarns
20 g/¾ oz polyester toy filling

Size 3 mm (US 2/3) knitting needles
Size 3.25 mm (US D-3) crochet hook
A yarn needle to sew your work together
An embroidery needle
A red colouring pencil for colouring the cheeks

Doll

Head

The head pieces are knitted from the chin up to the forehead.

Back
Make 1
◊ Using size 3 mm (US 2/3) needles, cast on 13 sts in cream.
◊ First row: Inc1, K to last 2 sts, inc1, K1. (15 sts)
◊ Next row: P.
◊ Next row: K2, M1, K to last 2 sts, M1, K2. (17 sts)
◊ Work 5 rows in st st, beg with a P row.
◊ Break cream yarn and join rust yarn.
◊ Work 8 rows in st st, beg with a P row.
◊ Next row: K2, k2tog, K to last 4 sts, ssk, K2. (15 sts)
◊ Next row: P2tog, P to last 2 sts, p2tog. (13 sts)
◊ Rep last 2 rows once more. (9 sts)
◊ Cast off.

Front
Make 1
◊ Using size 3 mm (US 2/3) needles, cast on 13 sts in cream.
◊ First row: Inc1, K to last 2 sts, inc1, K1. (15 sts)
◊ Next row: P.
◊ Next row: K2, M1, K to last 2 sts, M1, K2. (17 sts)
◊ Work 7 rows in st st, beg with a K row.
◊ Next row: K8, K into f and b of next st, turn work and P2, turn again and K to end. (18 sts)
◊ Next row: P8, p2tog, P8. (17 sts)
◊ Work 4 rows in st st, beg with a K row.
◊ Next row: K2, k2tog, K to last 4 sts, ssk, K2. (15 sts)
◊ Next row: P2tog, P to last 2 sts, p2tog. (13 sts)
◊ Rep last 2 rows once more. (9 sts)
◊ Cast off.

Body

The body is knitted from the lower edge to the neck edge.

Make 2
◊ Using size 3 mm (US 2/3) needles, cast on 16 sts in pale pink.
◊ Work 6 rows in st st, beg with a K row.
◊ Break pale pink yarn and join mid-pink yarn.
◊ K 2 rows.
◊ Work 12 rows in st st, beg with a K row.
◊ Next row: Cast off 1 st kwise, K to end. (15 sts)
◊ Next row: Cast off 1 st pwise, P to end. (14 sts)
◊ Cast off.

Legs & feet

The legs and feet are knitted as one piece, from the sole of the foot to the top of the thigh.

Make 2
◊ Using size 3 mm (US 2/3) needles, cast on 24 sts in cream.
◊ Work 4 rows in st st, beg with a K row.
◊ Next row: K6, cast off 12 sts, K to end. (12 sts)
◊ Work 3 rows in st st, beg with a P row.
◊ Break cream yarn and join pale pink yarn.
◊ K 2 rows.
◊ Work 18 rows in st st, beg with a K row.
◊ Cast off.

Arms

The arms are knitted from the top of the shoulder to the tip of the hand.

Make 2
◊ Using size 3 mm (US 2/3) needles, cast on 9 sts in cream.
◊ Work 20 rows in st st, beg with a K row.
◊ Next row: K4, inc1, turn work, P2, turn work again, K to end. (10 sts)
◊ Next row: P4, p2tog, P4. (9 sts)
◊ Work 2 rows in st st, beg with a K row.
◊ Next row: K2, k2tog, K1, ssk, K2. (7 sts)
◊ Next row: P2tog, P3, p2tog. (5 sts)
◊ Cast off.

Making up

With the head pieces RS together, oversew around the sides and chin. Turn the head RS out through the top and stuff. Seam the top of the head, using mattress stitch.

Working from the lower edge of the body pieces, join one of the side seams, the top seam and then the other side seam using mattress stitch. Stuff the body, then close the lower edge, using mattress stitch.

With the leg and foot piece RS together, oversew the lower, back and top seams of the foot. Turn the piece RS out and sew the back leg seam, using mattress stitch. Stuff carefully. Complete the second leg in the same way.

With the arm piece RS together, oversew around the hand. Turn the arm RS out and sew the main seam, using mattress stitch. Complete the second arm in the same way. Do not stuff the arms.

Join the arms to the top edges of the main body and the legs to the outer edges of the lower body using mattress stitch. Using the same technique, fasten the head to the body at the back and just under the chin. The face should overlap the top part of the body by about 1 cm (³/₈ in).

Using black yarn, embroider two French knots for the eyes. Using white yarn, work a ring of chain stitch around each French knot. Separate a short length of black yarn lengthways so that you have two strands. Use one strand to work a few straight stitches around the eyes for the eyelashes. Using red yarn, work two straight stitches in a flattened V shape for the mouth. Use the red pencil to colour the cheeks.

For the front of the hair, work a few rows of chain stitch in rust yarn, side by side, from one side of the head to the centre of the top of the head. Do the same on the other side. For the plait, cut three 45-cm (16-in) lengths of rust yarn. Tie a 15-cm (6-in) length of yarn around the middle of the three long pieces of yarn and use this shorter yarn to attach the three longer pieces to the top of the head. Plait the yarn and secure the end by tying a simple knot.

Pullover sleeves

The main part of the pullover is knitted as part of the doll, so you only need to knit the sleeves.

Make 2
◊ Using size 3 mm (US 2/3) needles, cast on 13 sts in mid-pink.
◊ Work 13 rows in st st, beg with a K row.
◊ Next row: K.
◊ Cast off.

Making up

Fold the sleeves WS together and sew the side seams, using mattress stitch.
  Oversew the top of the sleeves around the very top of the arms and, if you like, roll the sleeves up the arms slightly.

Boots

Make 2
◊ Using size 3 mm (US 2/3) needles, cast on 26 sts in dark grey.
◊ K 2 rows.
◊ Work 4 rows in st st, beg with a K row.
◊ Next row: K7, cast off 12 sts, K to end. (14 sts)
◊ Work 5 rows in st st, beg with a P row.
◊ Next row: K.
◊ Cast off loosely.

Making up

Fold the pieces widthways, RS together. Oversew the back, lower and upper seams, then turn the boots RS out.

Dress

Back

Make 1
◊ Using size 3 mm (US 2/3) needles, cast on 15 sts in denim blue.
◊ K 2 rows.
◊ Next row: K2, P11, K2.
◊ Next row: K.
◊ Next row: K2, P11, K2.
◊ Rep last 2 rows 6 times more.
◊ Break yarn and leave sts on stitch holder or spare needle.

Front

Right side
Make 1
◊ Using size 3 mm (US 2/3) needles, cast on 4 sts in denim blue.
◊ First row: K2, inc1, K1. (5 sts)

- ◊ Next row: K2, P1, K2.
- ◊ Next row: K.
- ◊ Next row: K2, M1 pwise, P to last 2 sts, K2. (6 sts)
- ◊ Rep last 2 rows 6 times more (12 sts)
- ◊ Break yarn and leave sts on stitch holder or spare needle.

Left side
Make 1
- ◊ Using size 3 mm (US 2/3) needles, cast on 4 sts in denim blue.
- ◊ First row: Inc1, K3. (5 sts)
- ◊ Next row: K2, P1, K2.
- ◊ Next row: K2, M1, K to end. (6 sts)
- ◊ Next row: K2, P to last 2 sts, K2.
- ◊ Rep last 2 rows 6 times more (12 sts)

Join pieces
- ◊ Next row: K2, M1, K10 from second side; with RS of back facing, K across 15 sts, then with RS of first side facing, K across 12 sts. (40 sts)
- ◊ Next row: K2, M1 pwise, P to last 2 sts, K2. (41 sts)
- ◊ Next row: K.
- ◊ Next row: K2, P to last 2 sts, K2.
- ◊ Rep last 2 rows 8 times more.
- ◊ K 2 rows.
- ◊ Cast off pwise.

Bow

Make 1
- ◊ Using a size 3.25 mm (US D-3) crochet hook, crochet a 15-cm (6-in) chain in denim blue.

Making up

Join the front shoulders to the back by oversewing about 5 mm ($\frac{1}{4}$ in). Place the dress on the doll and overlap the right side of the front over the left. Stitch the centre of the crochet chain for the bow at the side waist. Tie in a bow.

Headscarf

Make 1
- ◊ Using size 3 mm (US 2/3) needles, cast on 30 sts in bright green.
- ◊ K 2 rows.
- ◊ Next row: P2tog, P to last 2 sts, p2tog.
- ◊ Next row: K.
- ◊ Rep last 2 rows 12 times (4 sts)
- ◊ Next row: [P2tog] twice.
- ◊ Next row: K2tog.
- ◊ Break yarn and pull it through rem st.

Scarf ties

Make 2
- ◊ Using a size 3.25 mm (US D-3) crochet hook, crochet a 7-cm ($2\frac{3}{4}$-in) chain in bright green.

Making up

Use the yarn tails at the end of the chains to fasten the ties to the two sides of the headscarf. Trim and fray the free ends of the chains.

Cockerel & hen

Strutting about, shaking their tail feathers – and usually making something of a din – hens and cockerels are some of the most striking creatures on the farm. They are knitted here in some fairly traditional hues, but the colour choices are up to you. And if your fingers are feeling nifty, don't forget to complete your loving couple by knitting them a few tiny eggs.

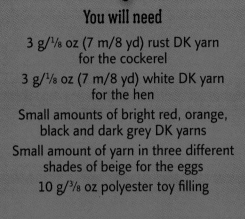

Doll (for both)

Body & head

Side 1

Make 1

◊ Using size 3 mm (US 2/3) needles, cast on 4 sts in rust (white).
◊ First row: Inc1, K1, inc1, K1. (6 sts)
◊ Next row: P.
◊ Next row: [Inc1] twice, K1, [inc1] twice, K1. (10 sts)
◊ Next row: P.
◊ Next row: [Inc1] twice, K5, [inc1] twice, K1. (14 sts)
◊ Next row: P.
◊ Next row: Inc1, K to end. (15 sts)
◊ Next row: P.
◊ Rep last 2 rows twice more. (17 sts)
◊ Next row: Cast off 9 sts pwise, K to end. (8 sts)
◊ Next row: P.
◊ For cockerel only: Break rust yarn and join black yarn.
◊ Cockerel and hen next row: K1, k2tog, K to end. (7 sts)
◊ Next row: P.
◊ Rep last 2 rows once more. (6 sts)
◊ Next row: K1, k2tog, ssk, K1. (4 sts)
◊ Next row: [P2tog] twice. (2 sts)
◊ Next row: K2tog. (1 st)
◊ Break yarn and pull it through rem st.

Side 2

Make 1

◊ Using size 3 mm (US 2/3) needles, cast on 4 sts in rust (white).
◊ First row: Inc1, K1, inc1, K1. (6 sts)
◊ Next row: P.
◊ Next row: [Inc1] twice, K1, [inc1] twice, K1. (10 sts)
◊ Next row: P.
◊ Next row: [Inc1] twice, K5, [inc1] twice, K1. (14 sts)
◊ Next row: P.
◊ Next row: K to last 2 sts, inc1, K1. (15 sts)
◊ Next row: P.
◊ Rep last 2 rows twice more. (17 sts)
◊ Next row: K.
◊ Next row: Cast off 9 sts kwise, P to end. (8 sts)
◊ For cockerel only: Break rust yarn and join black yarn.
◊ Cockerel and hen next row: K to last 3 sts, ssk, K1. (7 sts)
◊ Next row: P.
◊ Rep last 2 rows once more. (6 sts)
◊ Next row: K1, k2tog, ssk, K1. (4 sts)
◊ Next row: [P2tog] twice. (2 sts)
◊ Next row: K2tog. (1 st)
◊ Break yarn and pull it through rem st.

Wings

Make 2

◊ Using size 3 mm (US 2/3) needles, cast on 4 sts in rust (white).
◊ Work 6 rows in st st, beg with a K row.
◊ Next row: K2tog, ssk. (2 sts)
◊ Next row: P2tog. (1 st)
◊ Break yarn and pull it through rem st.

Tail feathers

Make 1 set

◊ For the cockerel, cut five 12-cm (4¾-in) lengths of black yarn and four lengths of rust yarn.
◊ For the hen, cut seven 12-cm (4¾-in) lengths of white yarn and two lengths of dark grey yarn.
◊ Gather together and secure around the middle with a length of matching yarn.

Comb

Make 1

◊ Separate a length of red yarn into two strands.
◊ Using size 2.25 mm (US 1) needles, cast on 4 sts in one strand of red yarn.

◊ First row: Cast off 2 sts (1 st on RH needle), K1. (2 sts)
◊ Next row: K.
◊ Next row: Cast on 2 sts, cast off 2 sts (1 st on RH needle), K1. (2 sts)
◊ Next row: K.
◊ Next row: Cast on 2 sts, cast off all rem sts.

Making up

With the two body sides RS together, oversew around each bird, leaving the base open for turning and stuffing. Turn the birds RS out, stuff and then sew the gap closed.

For the cockerel, using a split length of black yarn, work a number of vertical straight stitches just below the base of the black neck, using the photograph as a guide.

Secure the wings by oversewing the top and bottom of the front part of the wing to the body; the outer edges of the wings should be free.

Sew each comb in place on top of the head. Using a split length of red yarn, work two small loops just below the beaks for the wattles.

Dampen the tail feather yarns and separate some of the strands. Secure at the tail end of each bird and trim the strands.

Split a length of black yarn into two strands and use these to work two French knots for the eyes. Split a short length of cream yarn into two strands and use these to work a circle of chain stitch around the eyes of the cockerel. Do the same for the hen, using a short length of beige yarn. Using a single separated strand of black yarn, work three straight lines above the hen's eyes to represent eyelashes.

Using a separated length of orange yarn, make a French knot for the beak, winding the yarn three times around the needle instead of twice.

Eggs

Make 3, each in a different shade of beige
◊ Separate a length of beige yarn into two strands.
◊ Using size 2.25 mm (US 1) needles, cast on 3 sts in one strand of beige yarn.
◊ First row: [Inc1] 3 times. [6 sts]
◊ Next and every WS row: P.
◊ Next RS row: [Inc1] 6 times. [12 sts]
◊ Next RS row: K.

◊ Next RS row: K2tog, K3, k2tog, K3, ssk. [9 sts]
◊ Next RS row: [K2tog] twice, K1, [ssk] twice. [5 sts]
◊ Next RS row: K2tog, K1, ssk. [3 sts]
◊ Break yarn and thread it through rem sts.

Making up

Fold the piece lengthways, with RS together, and oversew half way up the main seam. Turn the piece RS out and stuff lightly. Finish sewing the seam, using mattress stitch.

Morning: milking the cows

While Anna makes them both a hot drink, Frank's bringing the cows in for their early-morning milking. Although on cold winter days the herd stays snug in the barn, through spring and summer they're out in the fields grazing on the fresh grass, so they have to be collected and taken back to the barn to be milked twice a day.

Cow

Cows graze the fields all day long and provide us with beef and milk. This sweet-natured dairy cow, complete with udder, is knitted in a smooth, tan yarn – but if you fancy knitting one in a different colour or in a fuzzier yarn, then the choice is yours.

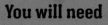

You will need

27 g/1 oz (68 m/74 yd) tan DK yarn
Small amounts of white, pale pink and rust yarn
Very small amounts of black, pale grey and dark pink DK yarns
40 g/1^1/$_2$ oz polyester toy filling

Size 3 mm (US 2/3) knitting needles
Size 3.25 mm (US D-3) crochet hook
A yarn needle to sew your work together
An embroidery needle

Doll

Head

Make 1

◊ Using size 3 mm (US 2/3) needles, cast on 34 sts in tan.
◊ Work 8 rows in st st, beg with a K row.
◊ Next row: K3, k2tog, K5, k2tog, K10, ssk, K5, ssk, K3. (30 sts)
◊ Next row: P.
◊ Next row: K3, k2tog, K4, k2tog, K8, ssk, K4, ssk, K3. (26 sts)
◊ Next row: P2tog, P22, p2tog. (24 sts)
◊ Next row: K5, k2tog, K3, k2tog, ssk, K3, ssk, K5. (20 sts)
◊ Work 5 rows in st st, beg with a P row.
◊ K 2 rows.
◊ Break tan yarn and join pale pink yarn.
◊ Work 2 rows in st st, beg with a K row.
◊ Next row: [K2tog] 5 times, [ssk] 5 times. (10 sts)
◊ Break pale pink yarn and thread it through rem sts.

Body

Make 1

◊ Using size 3 mm (US 2/3) needles, cast on 42 sts in tan.
◊ Work 8 rows in st st, beg with a K row.
◊ Next row: K3, M1, K to last 3 sts, M1, K3. (44 sts)
◊ Work 3 rows in st st, beg with a P row.
◊ Rep last 4 rows 3 times more. (50 sts)
◊ Next row: K3, k2tog, K to last 5 sts, ssk, K3. (48 sts)
◊ Work 3 rows in st st, beg with a P row.
◊ Rep last 4 rows twice more. (44 sts)
◊ Next row: K3, k2tog, K to last 5 sts, ssk, K3. (42 sts)
◊ Work 2 rows in st st, beg with a P row.
◊ Next row: P2tog, P to last 2 sts, p2tog. (40 sts)
◊ Next row: K2, [k2tog] twice, K to last 6 sts, [ssk] twice, K2. (36 sts)
◊ Next row: P2tog, P to last 2 sts, p2tog. (34 sts)
◊ Next row: K2, k2tog, K3, [k2tog] 5 times, [ssk] 5 times, K3, ssk, K2. (22 sts)
◊ Next row: P2tog, P to last 2 sts, p2tog. (20 sts)
◊ Cast off.

Back legs

Make 2

◊ Using size 3 mm (US 2/3) needles, cast on 9 sts in tan.
◊ K 2 rows.
◊ Work 12 rows in st st, beg with a K row.
◊ Next row: K2, M1, K5, M1, K2. (11 sts)
◊ Work 3 rows in st st, beg with a P row.
◊ Next row: K2, M1, K to last 2 sts, M1, K2. (13 sts)
◊ Next row: P.

◊ Rep last 2 rows 3 times more. (19 sts)
◊ Work 4 rows in st st, beg with a K row.
◊ Next row: K1, k2tog, K13, ssk, K1. (17 sts)
◊ Next row: P2tog, P13, p2tog. (15 sts)
◊ Cast off.

Front legs

Make 2
◊ Using size 3 mm (US 2/3) needles, cast on 9 sts in white.
◊ K 2 rows.
◊ Work 8 rows in st st, beg with a K row.
◊ Break white yarn and join tan yarn.
◊ Work 8 rows in st st, beg with a K row.
◊ Next row: K2, M1, K to last 2 sts, M1, K2. (11 sts)
◊ Work 3 rows in st st, beg with a P row.
◊ Rep last 4 rows once more. (13 sts)
◊ Work 4 rows in st st, beg with a K row.
◊ Cast off.

Udder

Make 1
◊ Using size 3 mm (US 2/3) needles, cast on 26 sts in pale pink.
◊ Work 6 rows in st st, beg with a K row.
◊ Next row: [K1, k2tog] 8 times, K2. (18 sts)
◊ Next row: [P2tog] 9 times. (9 sts)
◊ Break yarn and thread it through rem sts.

Ears

Make 2
◊ Using size 3 mm (US 2/3) needles, cast on 5 sts in tan.
◊ Work 5 rows in st st, beg with a K row.
◊ Next row: P2tog, P1, p2tog. (3 sts)
◊ Next row: S1, k2tog, psso. (1 st)
◊ Break yarn and pull it through rem st.

Tail

Make 1
◊ Using a size 3.25 mm (US D-3) crochet hook and a double strand of yarn, crochet a 5-cm (2-in) chain in tan yarn.
◊ Pull firmly at the end and trim to form part of the switch.
◊ Tie on two short lengths of rust yarn to add to the switch.

Making up

Pull the yarn tail at the end of the nose fairly tightly and secure. Use the yarn tail to sew the pink part of the nose. Complete the seam, which will run down the back of the head, using a tan yarn tail. Leave the back edge open for stuffing. Stuff the head, then close the gap, using mattress stitch.

For the eyes, work two French knots using black yarn. Using white yarn, work a circle of chain stitch around each French knot. Using a separated strand of black yarn, work three short straight stitches above each eye for the eyelashes. Using pale grey yarn, work two French knots for the nostrils and using dark pink yarn work a couple of straight stitches in a flattened V shape for the mouth.

Pinch the ears at the bottom and oversew them in position on the side of the head.

Fold the body piece in half with RS outwards and seam the front and lower seams using mattress stitch. Stuff the body fairly firmly, then use mattress stitch to close the back seam.

Oversew the head to the body.

Fold each of the legs in half lengthways with RS together and oversew the hooves. Turn the legs RS out and sew the side seams using mattress stitch. Stuff the legs and oversew to the body.

Sew the side seam of the udder using mattress stitch. Stuff lightly and oversew in place. Using pale pink yarn, work four French knots for the nipples, winding the yarn three times around the needle instead of twice.

Attach the tail.

Sew a few pieces of rust yarn to the top of the head for the forelock and separate the strands.

Horse

Tall and haughty and very fond of swishing his long tail, this horse is a little too smart to drag a plough around in the way his ancestors did. He'd much prefer to prance about in a field and boss the other animals around! He's knitted here in a traditional, soft brown woollen yarn, but you could also try pale grey or caramel to transform him into a different breed.

You will need

22 g/³/₄ oz (54 m/59 yd) soft brown DK yarn

3.5 g/¹/₈ oz (8 m/9 yd) dark brown DK yarn

A small amount of black DK yarn

Very small amounts of white, beige and pale pink DK yarns

40 g/1¹/₂ oz polyester toy filling

Size 3 mm (US 2/3) knitting needles

Size 2.75 mm (US 2) knitting needles

A yarn needle to sew your work together

An embroidery needle

Doll

Body & head

Make 1

◊ Using size 3 mm (US 2/3) needles, cast on 16 sts in soft brown.
◊ Next row: [Inc1] twice, K to end. (18 sts)
◊ Next row: P.
◊ Rep last 2 rows 3 times more. (24 sts)
◊ Work 12 rows in st st, beg with a K row.
◊ Next row: [K2tog] twice, K to end. (22 sts)
◊ Next row: P.
◊ Mark beg and end of last row with a small safety pin or piece of yarn. These mark the neck and rear end of the top of the horse's back.
◊ Next row: [Inc1] twice, K to end. (24 sts)
◊ Work 13 rows in st st, beg with a P row.
◊ Next row: [Ssk] twice, K to end. (22 sts)
◊ Next row: P.
◊ Rep last 2 rows 3 times more. (16 sts)
◊ Cast off.
◊ With the RS of your work facing you, pick up and K 22 sts from the outer corner of the straight edge (across the row ends) to the central safety pin or yarn marker. Turn work, cast on 46 sts. (68 sts)

◊ Next row: P2tog, P to last 2 sts, p2tog. (66 sts)
◊ Next row: K.
◊ Rep last 2 rows 3 times more. (60 sts)
◊ Next row: P2tog, P to last 2 sts, p2tog. (58 sts)
◊ Next row: Cast off 20 sts kwise, K to end. (38 sts)
◊ Next row: Cast off 20 sts pwise, P to end. (18 sts)
◊ Work 5 rows in st st, beg with a K row.
◊ Next row: K.
◊ Work 4 rows in st st, beg with a K row.
◊ Next row: [K2tog] 4 times, K2, [ssk] 4 times. (10 sts)
◊ Next row: [P2tog] 5 times. (5 sts)
◊ Break yarn, thread it through rem sts and secure.

Back legs

Make 2

◊ Using size 3 mm (US 2/3) needles, cast on 8 sts in black.
◊ K 4 rows.
◊ Break black yarn and join soft brown yarn.
◊ Work 14 rows in st st, beg with a K row.
◊ Next row: K2, M1, K4, M1, K2. (10 sts)
◊ Work 3 rows in st st, beg with a P row.

◊ Next row: K2, M1, K to last 2 sts, M1, K2. (12 sts)
◊ Next row: P.
◊ Rep last 2 rows 3 times more. (18 sts)
◊ Work 4 rows in st st, beg with a K row.
◊ Next row: K1, k2tog, K12, ssk, K1. (16 sts)
◊ Next row: P2tog, P to last 2 sts, p2tog. (14 sts)
◊ Cast off.

Front legs

Make 2
◊ Using size 3 mm (US 2/3) needles, cast on 8 sts in black.
◊ K 4 rows.
◊ Break black yarn and join soft brown yarn.
◊ Work 14 rows in st st, beg with a K row.
◊ Next row: K1, M1, K6, M1, K1. (10 sts)
◊ Work 5 rows in st st, beg with a P row.
◊ Next row: K1, M1, K8, M1, K1. (12 sts)
◊ Work 3 rows in st st, beg with a P row.
◊ Next row: K1, k2tog, K6, ssk, K1. (10 sts)
◊ Next row: P2tog, P6, p2tog. (8 sts)
◊ Cast off.

Ears

Make 2
◊ Using size 2.75 mm (US 2) needles, cast on 5 sts in soft brown.
◊ K 4 rows.
◊ Next row: K2tog, K3. (4 sts)
◊ Next row: K2tog, ssk. (2 sts)
◊ Next row: K2tog. (1 st)
◊ Break yarn and pull it through rem st.

Making up

Fold the head and body piece so that the head part is RS together and oversew the seam along the lower edge of the head. Turn the piece RS out and sew the front of the neck using mattress stitch. Using mattress stitch, join the unattached side of the lower neck to the unattached side of the body.

Join the seam at the back of the neck and the back end of the horse using mattress stitch. Stuff the body and head, then close the gap along the lower edge using mattress stitch.

Fold the front leg pieces lengthways, WS together. Oversew the lower and side seams of the hooves, then join the long seams using mattress stitch, leaving the top edge open for stuffing. Stuff and oversew in place.

Fold the back leg pieces lengthways, RS together. Oversew the seam on the top part of the legs, leaving the top edge open for stuffing. Turn RS out and sew the lower part of the seam using mattress stitch. Oversew the lower and side seams of the hooves. Stuff and oversew in place.

Using black yarn, work a row of chain stitch around the top of each hoof.

For the eyes, work two French knots using black yarn. Using white yarn, work two circles of chain stitch around each French knot. Using beige yarn, work two French knots for the nostrils. Using white yarn, work a row of chain stitch for the teeth. Using pale pink yarn, work two straight stitches above the teeth for the mouth. Oversew the ears in position.

For the mane and forelock, cut thirty 8-cm (3-in) lengths of dark brown yarn. Working with two strands at a time, using matching yarn, back stitch the centre of the strands along the back of the neck and up to the forehead. Dampen the yarn and separate the strands to give it a more natural look. Trim.

For the tail, cut ten 25-cm (10-in) lengths of dark brown yarn and gather them together into a bunch. Secure the centre of the bunch in position at the end of the horse, using a separate piece of yarn. Wrap the yarn a few times around the bottom of the bunch. To give the tail a tousled look, dampen it and separate some of the strands. Trim.

Lunchtime: break for lunch

Frank and Anna have been up since dawn,
so at noon they take an early break for lunch.
The sun's up and it's a lovely day, so they
take a picnic out to the hayfield and
lean back comfortably in the shade of
a haystack. Bess the collie has come
along for the break. She's always
hopeful of getting a few scraps
from a sandwich or some crumbs
of cookie.

Play mat

When you have completed your farmer and his wife and knitted all the creatures, you'll obviously need to create a special play area for them. The play mat is made up of six different rectangles or 'fields'. The fields are then sewn together and a crochet border is worked around the entire piece. You can easily make the mat larger than shown here by creating extra fields. You can also mix and match the fields and arrange them in any way you like.

You will need

23 g/1 oz (57 m/62 yd) bright green DK yarn

23 g/1 oz (57 m/62 yd) sage green DK yarn

8 g/$\frac{1}{4}$ oz (20 m/22 yd) aqua DK yarn

4 g/$\frac{1}{8}$ oz (10 m/11 yd) mid-green DK yarn (for the pond edge and for the crochet border around the mat)

23 g/1 oz (57 m/62 yd) flecked green DK yarn

23 g/1 oz (57 m/62 yd) pale green DK yarn

28 g/1 oz (70 m/77 yd) dark brown DK yarn

28 g/1 oz (70 m/77 yd) pale brown DK yarn

Very small amounts of dark red and bright yellow DK yarns for the embroidered flowers

Size 3.25 mm (US 3) knitting needles

Size 4.25 mm (US G-6) crochet hook

A yarn needle to sew your work together

An embroidery needle

Note

Because the fields are worked in different stitches and you may be using different yarn brands for the different fields, the number of rows you need to knit for each field may vary slightly. The easiest way to allow for this is to start your play mat by knitting the cabbage patch. Once this is complete, you can simply knit all the other fields to the same length.

Cabbage patch

Make 1

◊ Using size 3.25 (US 3) needles, cast on 45 sts in bright green.
◊ Work 10 rows in st st, beg with a K row.
◊ Next row: K8, mb, [K6, mb] 4 times, K8.
◊ Work 9 rows in st st, beg with a P row.
◊ Rep last 10 rows 4 times more.
◊ Work 2 rows in st st, beg with a K row.
◊ Cast off.

Field with pond

Make 1

◊ Using size 3.25 mm (US 3) needles, cast on 45 sts in sage green.
◊ Beg with a K row, work in st st until the field measures the same as the cabbage patch, ending with a P row.
◊ Cast off.

Pond

Make 1

◊ Using size 3.25 mm (US 3) needles, cast on 23 sts in aqua.
◊ First row: K5, [P1, K5] to end.
◊ Next row: K1, [P3, K3] to last 4 sts, P3, K1.
◊ Next row: P2, [K1, P2] to end.
◊ Next row: P1, [K3, P3] to last 4 sts, K3, P1.
◊ Next row: K2, [P1, K5] to last 3 sts, P1, K2.
◊ Next row: P.
◊ Rep these 6 rows 6 times more.
◊ Cast off.

Making up

Oversew the pond in the centre of the field. Using two strands of mid-green yarn, work a border of chain stitch around the pond.

Embroider the flowers in one corner of the field, using dark red yarn for the lazy daisy stitch petals and making French knots in bright yellow yarn for the flower centres.

Floral field

Make 1

◊ Using size 3.25 mm (US 3) needles, cast on 45 sts in flecked green.
◊ Beg with a K row, work in st st until the field measures the same as the cabbage patch, ending with a P row.
◊ Cast off.

Seeded field

Make 1

◊ Using size 3.25 mm (US 3) needles, cast on 45 sts in pale green.
◊ First row: P1, [K3, P1] to end.
◊ Next row: P.
◊ Next row: K.
◊ Next row: P.
◊ Next row: K2, P1, [K3, P1] to last 2 sts, K2.
◊ Next row: P.
◊ Next row: K.
◊ Next row: P.
◊ Rep these 8 rows until the field measures the same as the cabbage patch, ending with a P row.
◊ Cast off.

Ploughed field

◊ Using size 3.25 mm (US 3) needles, cast on 45 sts in dark brown.
◊ First row: K2, [P1, K3] to last 3 sts, P1, K2.
◊ Next row: P1, [K3, P1] to end.
◊ Rep these 2 rows until the field measures the same as the cabbage patch, ending after a second row.
◊ Cast off.

Rocky field

◊ Using size 3.25 mm (US 3) needles, cast on 46 sts in pale brown.
◊ First row: P.
◊ Next row: K1, *[K1, P1, K1] all into next st, p3tog, rep from * to last st, K1.
◊ Next row: P.
◊ Next row: K1, *p3tog, [K1, P1, K1] all into next st, rep from * to last st, K1.
◊ Rep these 4 rows until the field measures the same as the cabbage patch, after completing a row on the WS of your work.
◊ Cast off.

Making up

Join the fields together using the flat-seam technique (see page 15).

Using a size 4.25 mm (US G-6) crochet hook and a double strand of yarn, work a crochet edging (see page 16) in mid-green around the entire edge of the mat.

Afternoon: herding the sheep

It's mid-afternoon, and Frank needs to move
the sheep to a field with fresh grass. Bess
the collie enjoys helping, running around
the outside of the flock and rounding up any
stragglers. Just a few decide
that they don't want to join
the others, but Bess soon
sorts them out, and by the time the
sun starts to go down, they're all
enjoying the lush
pasture in their
new field.

Sheep & lamb

Sweet natured, docile and content to follow the crowd instead of blaze a trail, a warm, fuzzy sheep is hard to resist. This traditional-looking ewe and her little lamb are knitted in a textured fluffy wool yarn for some added authenticity. However, you could knit them in almost any DK yarn of your choice.

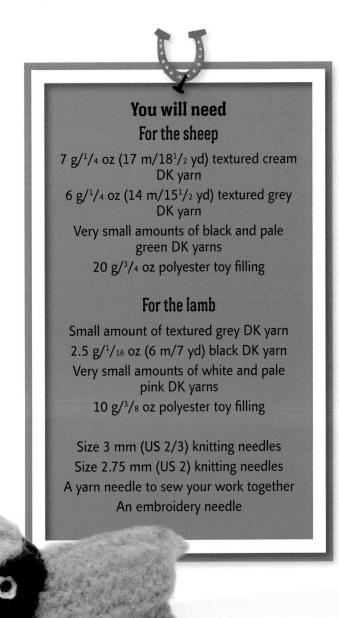

You will need
For the sheep
7 g/$^1/_4$ oz (17 m/18$^1/_2$ yd) textured cream DK yarn

6 g/$^1/_4$ oz (14 m/15$^1/_2$ yd) textured grey DK yarn

Very small amounts of black and pale green DK yarns

20 g/$^3/_4$ oz polyester toy filling

For the lamb
Small amount of textured grey DK yarn

2.5 g/$^1/_{16}$ oz (6 m/7 yd) black DK yarn

Very small amounts of white and pale pink DK yarns

10 g/$^3/_8$ oz polyester toy filling

Size 3 mm (US 2/3) knitting needles

Size 2.75 mm (US 2) knitting needles

A yarn needle to sew your work together

An embroidery needle

Sheep

Body

The body is knitted from the rear to the neck.

Make 1
◊ Using size 3 mm (US 2/3) needles, cast on 20 sts in cream.
◊ Work 6 rows in st st, beg with a K row.
◊ K 30 rows.
◊ Work 6 rows in st st, beg with a K row.
◊ Cast off.

Head

The head is knitted from the top of the head to the tip of the nose.

Make 1
◊ Using size 3 mm (US 2/3) needles, cast on 20 sts in grey.
◊ Work 14 rows in st st, beg with a K row.
◊ Next row: K2, [k2tog] twice, K2, k2tog, ssk, K2, [ssk] twice, K2. (14 sts)
◊ Next row: P2tog, P10, p2tog. (12 sts)
◊ Next row: [K2tog] 3 times, [ssk] 3 times. (6 sts)
◊ Break yarn and thread it through rem sts.

Legs

Make 4
◊ Using size 3 mm (US 2/3) needles, cast on 7 sts in grey.
◊ Work 8 rows in st st, beg with a K row.
◊ Break grey yarn and join cream yarn.
◊ K 2 rows.
◊ Next row: K1, M1, K5, M1, K1. (9 sts)
◊ K 2 rows.
◊ Cast off.

Ears

Make 2
◊ Using size 2.75 mm (US 2) needles, cast on 4 sts in grey.
◊ K 4 rows.
◊ Next row: K2tog, ssk. (2 sts)
◊ Next row: K2tog. (1 st)
◊ Break yarn and pull it through rem st.

Tail

Make 1
◊ Using size 3 mm (US 2/3) needles, cast on 8 sts in cream.
◊ K 1 row.
◊ Cast off.

Making up

Fold the head piece RS together and oversew the back seam, leaving the top open for turning and stuffing. Turn the head RS out and stuff. Make sure that the back seam is in the centre and close the top of the head using mattress stitch.

Fold the body piece in half widthways, with WS together. Seam the lower and back edges using mattress stitch, leaving the neck edge open for stuffing. Stuff the body. Oversew the head to the body. Oversew the ears in place.

Fold the tail in half lengthways in the way the piece naturally curls. Oversew the seam and stitch in place.

Fold the leg pieces lengthways, WS together. Oversew the short edges and join the long seams using mattress stitch, leaving the top edge open for stuffing. Stuff and stitch in place.

For the eyes, work two French knots using black yarn. Using pale green yarn, work a circle of chain stitch around each French knot. Using black yarn, work three straight stitches in a 'Y' shape for the nose and mouth. Using a single strand of black yarn, work three straight stitches above each eye to represent eyelashes. Add a few loops of yarn at the top of the head.

To give your sheep a fuzzy look, dampen her slightly and brush quite vigorously with a small nylon bristle brush.

Lamb

Body

Make 1
◊ Using size 3 mm (US 2/3) needles, cast on 15 sts in grey.
◊ Work 4 rows in st st, beg with a K row.
◊ K 20 rows.
◊ Work 4 rows in st st, beg with a K row.
◊ Cast off.

Head

Make 1
◊ Using size 3 mm (US 2/3) needles, cast on 18 sts in black.
◊ Work 8 rows in st st, beg with a K row.
◊ Next row: K2, k2tog, K2, k2tog, K2, ssk, K2, ssk, K2. (14 sts)
◊ Next row: P2tog, P10, p2tog. (12 sts)
◊ Next row: K1, [k2tog] twice, K2, [ssk] twice, K1. (8 sts)
◊ Next row: P2tog, P4, p2tog. (6 sts)
◊ Break yarn and thread it through rem sts.

Legs

Make 4
◊ Using size 3 mm (US 2/3) needles, cast on 6 sts in black.
◊ Work 4 rows in st st, beg with a K row.
◊ Break black yarn and join grey yarn.
◊ K 4 rows.
◊ Cast off.

Ears

Make 2
◊ Using size 2.75 mm (US 2) needles, cast on 4 sts in black.
◊ K 2 rows.
◊ Next row: K2tog, ssk. (2 sts)
◊ Next row: K2tog. (1 st)
◊ Break yarn and pull it through rem st.

Tail

Make 1
◊ Using size 3 mm (US 2/3) needles, cast on 6 sts in grey.
◊ K 1 row.
◊ Cast off.

Making up

The lamb is made up in the same way as the sheep, except for the facial features.

For the eyes, separate a length of cream yarn into two strands. Use one of these to work two small circles of chain stitch for the outer eye. Using black yarn, work a French knot in the centre of each chain-stitch circle. Using pink yarn, work three straight stitches in a 'Y' shape for the nose and mouth.

Bess the Collie

Energetic and agile, Bess is always ready for some playful bounding around. When work beckons, she's also happy to herd a few sheep. Knitted in two strands of mohair throughout and incorporating some interesting loopy stitches, this is one cute canine.

You will need

5 g/¼ oz (37 m/40½ yd) black mohair yarn

2 g/¹⁄₁₆ oz (13 m/14 yd) white mohair yarn

Very small amounts of dark pink, black and white DK yarns

15 g/½ oz polyester toy filling

Size 3 mm (US 2/3) knitting needles

Size 2.25 mm (US 1) knitting needles

A yarn needle to sew your work together

An embroidery needle

Doll

Body

Make 1

◊ Using size 3 mm (US 2/3) needles and a double strand of yarn, cast on 16 sts in black mohair.
◊ Work 10 rows in st st, beg with a K row.
◊ Next row: K2, M1, K12, M1, K2. (18 sts)
◊ Work 9 rows in st st, beg with a P row.
◊ Next row: K2, M1, K14, M1, K2. (20 sts)
◊ Work 5 rows in st st, beg with a P row.
◊ Next row: K2, M1, K16, M1, K2. (22 sts)
◊ Work 3 rows in st st, beg with a P row.
◊ Cast off.

Head

Make 1

◊ Using size 3 mm (US 2/3) needles and a double strand of yarn, cast on 20 sts in black mohair.
◊ Work 2 rows in st st, beg with a K row.
◊ Next row: K1, k2tog, K to last 3 sts, ssk, K1. (18 sts)
◊ Next row: P.
◊ Rep last 2 rows 6 times more. (6 sts)
◊ Break yarn, thread it through rem sts and secure.

Back legs

Make 2

◊ Using size 3 mm (US 2/3) needles and a double strand of yarn, cast on 7 sts in white mohair.
◊ K 4 rows.

◊ Break white yarn and join a double strand of black mohair.
◊ Next row: K2, M1, K3, M1, K2. (9 sts)
◊ Work 3 rows in st st, beg with a P row.
◊ Next row: K2, M1, K to last 2 sts, M1, K2. (11 sts)
◊ Next row: P.
◊ Rep last 2 rows once more. (13 sts)
◊ Next row: k2tog, K9, ssk. (11sts)
◊ Next row: p2tog, P7, p2tog. (9 sts)
◊ Cast off.

Front legs

Make 2

◊ Using size 3 mm (US 2/3) needles and a double strand of yarn, cast on 6 sts in white mohair.
◊ K 4 rows.
◊ Work 12 rows in st st, beg with a K row.
◊ Next row: K2, [loop1] twice, K2.
◊ Next row: P.
◊ Cast off.

Bib

The bib is worked from the chest edge to the nose.

Make 1

◊ Using size 3 mm (US 2/3) needles and a double strand of yarn, cast on 5 sts in white mohair.
◊ Work 10 rows in st st, beg with a K row.
◊ Next row: K1, [loop1] 3 times, K1.
◊ Next row: P.
◊ Next row: Cast on 8 sts, K to end. (13 sts)
◊ Next row: Cast on 8 sts, P to end. (21 sts)
◊ Next row: [K1, loop1] to last st, K1.
◊ Next row: P.
◊ Next row: [Loop1, K1] to last st, loop1.
◊ Next row: Cast off 8 sts (1 st on RH needle), K4, cast off 8 sts. (5 sts)

◊ Break yarn and rejoin to rem 5 sts on RS of work.
◊ Work 2 rows in st st, beg with a K row.
◊ Next row: K2tog, K1, ssk. (3 sts)
◊ Work 9 rows in st st, beg with a P row.
◊ Cast off.

Ears

Make 2

◊ Using size 2.25 mm (US 1) needles and a double strand of yarn, cast on 4 sts in black mohair.
◊ Work 2 rows in st st, beg with a K row.
◊ Next row: K2tog, ssk. (2 sts)
◊ Next row: P2tog. (1 st)
◊ Break yarn and pull it through rem st.

Tail

Make 1

◊ Using size 3 mm (US 2/3) needles and a double strand of yarn, cast on 4 sts in white mohair.
◊ Work 2 rows in st st, beg with a K row.
◊ Next row: K1, [loop1] twice, K1.
◊ Next row: P.
◊ Rep last 2 rows once more.
◊ Break white yarn and join a double strand of black mohair.
◊ Next row: K1, [loop1] twice, K1.
◊ Next row: P.
◊ Rep last 2 rows twice more.
◊ Cast off.

Making up

Sew the neck seam of the head, using mattress stitch. Stuff the head.

Using mattress stitch, join the lower and front seams of the body piece, leaving the back end open. Stuff the body and close the back end seam using mattress stitch. Oversew the neck edge of the head to the body, so that the neck forms a circle on the front of the body. Oversew the bib in place.

Sew the seam together for the front legs using mattress stitch and oversew them in place. Fold the back leg pieces RS together and oversew along the lower edge and the front of the foot. Turn RS out. Seam the rest of the leg piece, using mattress stitch, stuffing as you go. Oversew the legs in place.

Sew the ears in place.

Fold the tail piece in half lengthways, with WS together, and oversew the seam. Sew the tail in position.

Using black yarn, work two French knots for the eyes. Using white yarn, work a circle of chain stitch around each French knot. Using black yarn, work a circle of chain stitch for the end of the nose. Using white mohair yarn, work a circle of chain stitch up and down the nose and around the nose tip. Using dark pink yarn, work a straight stitch for the mouth.

Cut all loops on the tail, bib and front legs.

Max the Cat

A muddy field may not be the ideal home for a feline, but then Max isn't your typical prissy pussycat – he's a dab hand at keeping the rodents out of the food stores. Knit him in grey, as shown here, or try him out in a tweedy orange or pure white for a slightly different look.

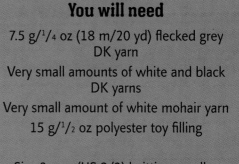

Doll

Body

The body is knitted from the rear to the neck.

Make 1
- Using size 3 mm (US 2/3) needles, cast on 12 sts in flecked grey.
- First row: Inc1, K to last 2 sts, inc1, K1. (14 sts)
- Work 3 rows in st st, beg with a P row.
- Next row: K2, M1, K to last 2 sts, M1, K2. (16 sts)
- Work 3 rows in st st, beg with a P row.
- Rep last 4 rows once more. (18 sts)
- Work 2 rows in st st, beg with a K row.
- Next row: K2, k2tog, K to last 4 sts, ssk, K2. (16 sts)
- Next row: P.
- Rep last 2 rows 3 times more. (10 sts)
- Next row: K2, k2tog, K to last 4 sts, ssk, K2. (8 sts)
- Cast off kwise.

Head

The head is knitted from the top of the head to the chin.

Make 1
- Using size 3 mm (US 2/3) needles, cast on 20 sts in flecked grey.
- Work 8 rows in st st, beg with a K row.
- Next row: K2, k2tog, K2, k2tog, K4, ssk, K2, ssk, K2. (16 sts)
- Next row: P2tog, P12, p2tog. (14 sts)
- Next row: [K2tog] 3 times, K2, [ssk] 3 times. (8 sts)
- Next row: P2tog, P4, p2tog. (6 sts)
- Cast off pwise.

Back legs

Make 2
- Using size 3 mm (US 2/3) needles, cast on 6 sts in flecked grey.
- Work 6 rows in st st, beg with a K row.
- Next row: K1, M1, K to last st, M1, K1. (8 sts)
- Next row: P.
- Rep last 2 rows once more. (10 sts)
- Work 2 rows in st st, beg with a K row.
- Next row: K2tog, K6, ssk. (8 sts)
- Cast off pwise.

Front legs

Make 2
- Using size 3 mm (US 2/3) needles, cast on 6 sts in flecked grey.
- Work 12 rows in st st, beg with a K row.
- Next row: K2tog, K2, ssk. (4 sts)
- Cast off pwise.

Tail

Make 1

◊ Using size 3 mm (US 2/3) needles, cast on 17 sts in flecked grey.
◊ Work 2 rows in st st, beg with a K row.
◊ Cast off.

Ears

Make 2

◊ Using size 2.75 mm (US 2) needles, cast on 4 sts in flecked grey.
◊ K 3 rows.
◊ Next row: K2tog, ssk. (2 sts)
◊ Next row: K2tog. (1 st)
◊ Break yarn and pull it through rem st.

Making up

Fold the head piece with RS together and oversew the back seam, leaving the top open for turning and stuffing. Turn the head RS out and stuff. Make sure the back seam is in the centre and close the top of the head using mattress stitch.

Fold the body piece in half widthways, with WS together. Seam the lower and back edges using mattress stitch, leaving the neck edge open for stuffing. Stuff the body. Oversew the head to the body.

Fold the tail in half lengthways in the way the piece naturally curls. Oversew the seam and stitch in place.

Fold the front leg pieces lengthways, with WS together. Oversew the lower edges and join the long seams using mattress stitch, leaving the top edge open for stuffing. Stuff and stitch in place.

Fold the back leg pieces lengthways, with RS together. Oversew the seam on the top part of the legs, leaving the top edge open for stuffing. Turn RS out and sew the lower part of the seam using mattress stitch and oversew the lower edges. Stuff and oversew in place.

For the eyes, work two French knots using black yarn. Using white yarn, work a circle of chain stitch around each French knot. Using black yarn, work a small triangle for the nose in satin stitch and work the mouth using straight stitch. Oversew the ears in position. Using a single strand of white mohair yarn, work three stitches on each side of the face to represent the whiskers.

To give your cat a fuzzy look, dampen him slightly and brush quite vigorously with a small nylon bristle brush.

Early Evening: touring the farm

It's early evening, and Frank and Anna go out together to tour the farm and check that all's well with the crops and animals. Frank picks an ear of corn – it's nearly ripe and soon it will be ready to be harvested – before Anna and Frank take it in turns to drive the tractor around and check all the fences and boundaries. Bess is busy chasing the pesky rabbits, and making sure they don't nibble Frank's precious crops.

Tractor

Specially designed to pull those heavy farm loads and agricultural machinery, tractors are essential farmyard vehicles. This squidgy, woolly version is somewhat different than its real-life counterpart – but it is much more fun to create.

You will need

19 g/⅝ oz (48 m/52½ yd) red DK yarn

17 g/½ oz (42 m/46 yd) black DK yarn

7 g/¼ oz (17 m/18½ yd) grey DK yarn

Small amounts of light silver metallicized crochet yarn and blue and olive green DK yarns

50 g/1¾ oz polyester toy filling

A piece of 3-mm (⅛-in) foam board (A5 size)

A bendable drinking straw

Size 3 mm (US 2/3) knitting needles

Size 2.75 mm (US 2) knitting needles

A yarn needle to sew your work together

Doll

Body

Make 1

◊ Using size 3 mm (US 2/3) needles, cast on 12 sts in red.
◊ Work 14 rows in st st, beg with a K row.
◊ Next row: Cast on 12 sts, K to end. (24 sts)
◊ Rep last row once more. (36 sts)
◊ Next row: K.
◊ Next row: P12, K1, P10, K1, P12.
◊ Rep last 2 rows 4 times more.
◊ Next row: K29, yf, k2tog, K5.
◊ Next row: P12, K1, P10, K1, P12.
◊ Next row: K.
◊ Next row: P12, K1, P10, K1, P12.
◊ Rep last 2 rows once more.
◊ K 4 rows.
◊ Next row: Cast off 12 sts kwise, K to end. (24 sts)
◊ Next row: Cast off 12 sts pwise, P to end. (12 sts)
◊ Next row: K.
◊ Next row: P3, K6, P3.
◊ Work 3 rows in st st, beg with a K row.
◊ Rep last 4 rows twice more.
◊ Next row: K.
◊ Work 18 rows in st st, beg with a K row.
◊ Cast off.

Base

Make 2 pieces

◊ Using size 3 mm (US 2/3) needles, cast on 14 sts in red.
◊ First row: K.
◊ Next row: K1, P to last st, K1.
◊ Rep last 2 rows 20 times more.
◊ Cast off.

Tyres

The tread of the tyres is knitted first and the two tyre sides are then knitted onto these.

Back tyres
Make 2

◊ Using size 3 mm (US 2/3) needles, cast on 7 sts in black.
◊ First row: K.
◊ Next row: P.
◊ K 2 rows.
◊ Rep last 4 rows 20 times more.
◊ Cast off.
◊ Pick up and K 42 sts along one side of the tread.
◊ First and every WS row unless stated otherwise: P.
◊ Next RS row: K.
◊ Next RS row: K2, [k2tog, K2] to end. (32 sts)
◊ Next RS row: K1, [k2tog, K2] to last 3 sts, k2tog, K1. (24 sts)
◊ Next RS row: [k2tog] to end. (12 sts)
◊ Next row: [P2tog] to end. (6 sts)
◊ Break yarn and thread it through rem sts.
◊ Rep on other side of the tread.

Front tyres
Make 2

◊ Using size 3 mm (US 2/3) needles, cast on 5 sts in black.
◊ First row: K.
◊ Next row: P.
◊ K 2 rows.
◊ Rep last 4 rows 11 times more.
◊ Pick up and K 24 sts along the side of the tread.
◊ First and every WS row unless stated otherwise: P.
◊ Next RS row: K1, [k2tog, K2] to last 3 sts, k2tog, K1. (18 sts)
◊ Next RS row: [K2tog] to end. (9 sts)

◊ Next row: [P2tog] twice, P1, [p2tog] twice. (5 sts)
◊ Break yarn and thread it through rem sts.
◊ Rep on other side of the tread.

Hubcaps

For the back wheels
Make 2
◊ Using size 3 mm (US 2/3) needles, cast on 24 sts
  in blue.
◊ First row: [K1, k2tog] to end. (16 sts)
◊ Next row: [P2tog] 8 times. (8 sts)
◊ Next row: [K2tog] 4 times. (4 sts)
◊ Break yarn and thread it through rem sts.

For the front wheels
Make 2
◊ Using size 3 mm (US 2/3) needles, cast on 18 sts
  in blue
◊ First row: [K1, k2tog] to end. (12 sts)
◊ Next row: [P2tog] 6 times. (6 sts)
◊ Next row: [K2tog] 3 times. (3 sts)
◊ Break yarn and thread it through rem sts.

Mudguards

**The mudguards over the back tyres are made
in two sections that are then sewn together.**

First section
Make 2
◊ Using size 3 mm (US 2/3) needles, cast on 20 sts
  in red.
◊ Work 2 rows in st st, beg with a K row.
◊ Next row: K2, k2tog, K to last 4 sts, ssk, K2.
  (18 sts)
◊ Next row: P.
◊ Rep last 2 rows once more. (16 sts)
◊ Next row: K2, k2tog, K to last 4 sts, ssk, K2. (14 sts)
◊ Next row: P2tog, P to last 2 sts, p2tog. (12 sts)

◊ Rep last 2 rows once more. (8 sts)
◊ Next row: K2tog, K to last 2 sts, ssk. (6 sts)
◊ Cast off pwise.

Second section
Make 2
◊ Using size 3 mm (US 2/3) needles, cast on 23 sts
  in red.
◊ First row: K2, P to last 2 sts, K2.
◊ Next row: K.
◊ Rep last 2 rows twice more.
◊ Next row: K2, P to last 2 sts, K2.
◊ Cast off.

Funnel

Make 1
◊ Using size 2.75 mm (US 2) needles, cast on 25 sts
  in light silver.
◊ Work 5 rows in st st, beg with a K row.
◊ Cast off kwise.

Seat

Main piece
**The main piece of the seat is
knitted from the bottom back
to the bottom front.**

Make 1
◊ Using size 3 mm (US 2/3)
  needles, cast on 12 sts
  in grey.
◊ Work 18 rows in
  st st, beg with
  a K row.
◊ P 2 rows.

◊ Work 2 rows in st st, beg with a K row.
◊ P 2 rows.
◊ Work 18 rows in st st, beg with a K row.
◊ P 2 rows.
◊ Work 8 rows in st st, beg with a K row.
◊ Cast off.

Side 1
Make 1
◊ Using size 3 mm (US 2/3) needles, cast on 5 sts in grey.
◊ Work 10 rows in st st, beg with a K row.
◊ Next row: Cast on 9 sts, K to end. (14 sts)
◊ Work 9 rows in st st, beg with a P row.
◊ Cast off.

Side 2
Make 1
◊ Using size 3 mm (US 2/3) needles, cast on 5 sts in grey.
◊ Work 9 rows in st st, beg with a K row.
◊ Next row: Cast on 9 sts, P to end. (14 sts)
◊ Work 9 rows in st st, beg with a K row.
◊ Cast off pwise.

Steering wheel

Make 2 pieces
◊ Using size 3 mm (US 2/3) needles, cast on 18 sts in olive green.
◊ First row: [K1, k2tog] to end. (12 sts)
◊ Next row: [P2tog] 6 times. (6 sts)
◊ Next row: [K2tog] 3 times. (3 sts)
◊ Break yarn and thread it through rem sts.

Making up

For the body, join the side seams to form a box shape, leaving one side open for stuffing. Stuff, then close the gap.

For the base, cut a piece of foam board measuring 11.5 x 4.25 cm (4$^{1}/_{2}$ in x 1$^{3}/_{4}$ in). With the two base pieces WS together, oversew around the two long and one short edge, keeping your stitching close to the edge. Insert the foam board and oversew the last side.

Oversew the body to one edge of the base.

For each wheel, you will need two circles of foam board. Cut out four circles 6.5 cm (2$^{1}/_{2}$ in) in diameter and four circles 4 cm (1$^{1}/_{2}$ in) in diameter. Sew the seams on one side of the tyre pieces to form a circle. Insert the two pieces of board and stuff the tyre between the two foam pieces. Seam the second side of the tyre. Complete the other wheels in the same way. Oversew the two sides of the hubcap pieces to form circles. Oversew the hubcaps in place. Sew the tyres in place. With the two mudguard pieces RS together, oversew the side piece to the longer strip and then oversew the mudguard in place on the tyre. Complete the second mudguard in the same way.

For the funnel, fold the piece in half lengthways, WS together, and oversew the short edge and a short length of the side seam. Insert the straw and complete the seam. Insert the funnel into the hole in the tractor body, securing with a few stitches if necessary.

For the seat, with WS together oversew the side pieces to the main piece to form a seat shape. Stuff the back of the seat, then work a line of running stitch along the seat where the back meets the seat part. Stuff the remainder of the seat. Sew the seat onto the tractor base.

Oversew the side seams of the two steering wheel pieces to form two circles. Place the two circles WS together and oversew around the edges. Sew the steering wheel in place by working a couple of small stitches through the centre of the wheel.

Pig & piglet

Pink and decidedly on the plump side, this pig is proud mother to a sweet little piglet and loves to have a good old sniff and trot around the farmyard. Knitted here in the gentlest shade of pale pink, this is a very traditional swine duo. But pigs come in all sorts of colours so, if you fancy it, you could knit your pigs in black or brown or even create a stripe around their middles.

You will need

For the pig

14 g/$\frac{1}{2}$ oz (32 m/35 yd) pale pink DK yarn

Very small amounts of black, cream, light grey and red DK yarns

15 g/$\frac{1}{2}$ oz polyester toy filling

For the piglet

3.5 g/$\frac{1}{8}$ oz (8 m/9 yd) pale pink DK yarn

Very small amounts of black, cream, light grey and bright pink DK yarns

5 g/$\frac{1}{4}$ oz polyester toy filling

Size 3 mm (US 2/3) knitting needles

Size 2.75 mm (US 2) knitting needles

Size 3.25 mm (US D-3) crochet hook

A yarn needle to sew your work together

An embroidery needle

Pig

Body

The body is knitted from the rear to the neck.

Make 1

◊ Using size 3 mm (US 2/3) needles, cast on 16 sts in pale pink.
◊ First row: Inc1, K13, inc1, K1. (18 sts)
◊ Next row: P.
◊ Next row: K2, M1, K to last 2 sts, M1, K2. (20 sts)
◊ Next row: P.
◊ Rep last 2 rows 6 times more. (32 sts)
◊ Work 8 rows in st st, beg with a K row.
◊ Next row: K2, [k2tog] twice, K20, [ssk] twice, K2. (28 sts)
◊ Next row: P2tog, P24, p2tog. (26 sts)
◊ Next row: K2, [k2tog] twice, K14, [ssk] twice, K2. (22 sts)
◊ Next row: P2tog, P to last 2 sts, p2tog. (20 sts)
◊ Work 2 rows in st st, beg with a K row.
◊ Cast off.

Head

The head is knitted in one piece, from the top of the head to the tip of the nose.

Make 1

◊ Using size 3 mm (US 2/3) needles, cast on 28 sts in pale pink.
◊ Work 4 rows in st st, beg with a K row.
◊ Next row: K4, [k2tog] 3 times, K8, [ssk] 3 times, K4. (22 sts)
◊ Work 3 rows in st st, beg with a P row.
◊ Next row: K6, k2tog, K6, s1, K1, psso, K6. (20 sts)
◊ Next row: P.
◊ Next row: K6, k2tog, K4, s1, K1, psso, K6. (18 sts)
◊ Next row: P.
◊ Next row: K2, k2tog, K4, k2tog, s1, K1, psso, K2, s1, K1, psso, K2. (14 sts)
◊ Next row: P.
◊ Next row: K2, k2tog, K6, s1, K1, psso, K2. (12 sts)
◊ K 2 rows.
◊ Break yarn, leaving a long tail. Thread the yarn tail through the rem sts.

Back legs

Make 2

◊ Using size 3 mm (US 2/3) needles, cast on 8 sts in pale pink.
◊ Work 6 rows in st st, beg with a K row.
◊ Next row: K1, M1, K to last st, M1, K1. (10 sts)
◊ Work 3 rows in st st, beg with a P row.
◊ Rep last 4 rows once more. (12 sts)
◊ Next row: K.
◊ Next row: P2tog, P to last 2 sts, p2tog. (10 sts)
◊ Cast off.

Front legs

Make 2
◊ Using size 3 mm (US 2/3) needles, cast on 8 sts in pale pink.
◊ Work 12 rows in st st, beg with a K row.
◊ Cast off.

Tail

Make 1
◊ Using a size 3.25 mm (US D-3) crochet hook, crochet a 4-cm (1¹/₂-in) crochet chain in pale pink.
◊ Trim and fray one end of the chain.

Ears

Make 2
◊ Using size 2.75 mm (US 2) needles, cast on 5 sts in pale pink.
◊ First row: Inc1, K2, inc1, K1. (7 sts)
◊ Next and every WS row: P.
◊ Next row: K2tog, K3, ssk. (5 sts)
◊ Next RS row: K2tog, K1, ssk. (3 sts)
◊ Next RS row: S1, k2tog, psso.
◊ Break yarn and pull it through rem st.

Making up

Run a line of running stitch along the neck edge of the body piece. Gather slightly and join to the neck edge of the head piece using mattress stitch. Fold the body and head piece in half lengthways, WS together, and sew the chin and lower body seam using mattress stitch, leaving the rear open for stuffing. Stuff the pig fairly firmly and close the gap using mattress stitch.

Fold the leg pieces lengthways, WS together. Oversew the short ends and join the long seams using mattress stitch, leaving the top edge open for stuffing. Stuff and oversew in place.

Make a loop in the tail to give it a curl and secure the curl with a couple of small stitches. Sew the tail in place.

Oversew the ears in place.

For the eyes, work two French knots using black yarn. Separate a length of cream yarn into two strands. Use these to work a circle of chain stitch around each French knot. Use a separated strand of black yarn to work three straight stitches for the eyelashes. Using light grey yarn, work two French knots for the nostrils. Use a separated strand of red yarn to work a couple of straight stitches, side by side, for the mouth.

Piglet

Body & head

Make 1
◊ Using size 3 mm (US 2/3) needles, cast on 10 sts in pale pink.
◊ First row: Inc1, K7, inc1, K1. (12 sts)
◊ Next row: P.
◊ Next row: K1, M1, K10, M1, K1. (14 sts)
◊ Work 9 rows in st st, beg with a P row.
◊ Next row: K1, M1, K12, M1, K1. (16 sts)
◊ Work 3 rows in st st, beg with a P row.
◊ Next row: K3, [k2tog] twice, K2, [ssk] twice, K3. (12 sts)
◊ Next row: P2tog, P8, p2tog. (10 sts)
◊ Next row: K2, k2tog, K2, ssk, K2. (8 sts)
◊ Next row: K2tog, K4, ssk. (6 sts)
◊ Next row: K.
◊ Break yarn, thread it through rem sts and secure.

Legs

Make 4
◊ Using size 3 mm (US 2/3) needles, cast on 5 sts in pale pink.
◊ Work 6 rows in st st, beg with a K row.
◊ Cast off.

Tail

Make 1
◊ Using a size 3.25 mm (US D-3) crochet hook, crochet a 4-cm (1$^1/_2$-in) crochet chain in pale pink.
◊ Trim one end of the chain and separate the strands to form the tail tip.

Ears

Make 2
◊ Using size 2.75 mm (US 2) needles, cast on 3 sts in pale pink.
◊ First row: K.
◊ Next row: P.
◊ Next row: K2tog, K1. (2 sts)
◊ Next row: P2tog. (1 st)
◊ Break yarn and pull it through rem st.

Making up

Sew the lower seam of the piglet using mattress stitch, leaving the rear open for stuffing. Stuff the piglet and close the gap, using mattress stitch.

Complete the rest of the piglet as for the pig, but omit the eyelashes and work the mouth in bright pink.

Dusk: a fox-eye view

As darkness falls, the animals are settling down for the night. At dusk, Frank goes off to do the day's second milking while Anna shuts the hens safely into their house. Just as well, because there's an uninvited visitor watching from above. A chicken dinner is the fox's favourite and he's disappointed to see that Anna isn't taking any chances. He lopes off to the farm over the hill; maybe he'll have better luck there.

Fox

Knitted in a beautiful shade of soft, rust-coloured yarn, this is one fine-looking fox. He may be sly. He may be scheming. He may be on a constant lookout for a tasty morsel of live poultry. But who could deny that he is handsome? 'Now on what page did I see that lovely hen?'

Doll

Body

The body is knitted from the rear to the neck.

Make 1
◊ Using size 3 mm (US 2/3) needles, cast on 12 sts in rust.
◊ First row: inc1, K9, inc1, K1. (14 sts)
◊ Work 3 rows in st st, beg with a P row.
◊ Next row: K2, M1, K to last 2 sts, M1, K2. (16 sts)
◊ Work 3 rows in st st, beg with a P row.
◊ Rep last 4 rows twice more. (20 sts)
◊ Work 6 rows in st st, beg with a K row.
◊ Next row: K2, [k2tog] twice, K8, [ssk] twice, K2. (16 sts)
◊ Next row: P2tog, P12, p2tog. (14 sts)
◊ Cast off.

Belly

Make 1
◊ Using size 2.75 m (US 1) needles and a double strand of yarn, cast on 5 sts in white mohair.
◊ Work 4 rows in st st, beg with a K row.
◊ Next row: K1, M1, K3, M1, K1. (7 sts)
◊ Work 3 rows in st st, beg with a P row.
◊ Next row: K1, M1, K to last st, M1, K1. (9 sts)
◊ Work 9 rows in st st, beg with a P row.

◊ Next row: K1, k2tog, K3, ssk, K1. (7 sts)
◊ Work 3 rows in st st, beg with a P row.
◊ Next row: K1, k2tog, K1, ssk, K1. (5 sts)
◊ Work 7 rows in st st, beg with a P row.
◊ Cast off.

Head

The head is knitted from the top of the head to the tip of the nose.

Make 1
◊ Using size 3 mm (US 2/3) needles, cast on 20 sts in rust.
◊ Work 8 rows in st st, beg with a K row.
◊ Next row: K2, k2tog, K2, k2tog, K4, ssk, K2, ssk, K2. (16 sts)
◊ Next row: P2tog, P12, p2tog. (14 sts)
◊ Next row: K2, [k2tog] twice, K2, [ssk] twice, K2. (10 sts)
◊ Next row: P2tog, P6, p2tog. (8 sts)
◊ Next row: [K2tog] twice, [ssk] twice. (4 sts)
◊ Cast off pwise.

Back legs

Make 2
◊ Using size 3 mm (US 2/3) needles, cast on 6 sts in rust.
◊ Work 8 rows in st st, beg with a K row.
◊ Next row: K1, M1, K to last st, M1, K1. (8 sts)
◊ Work 3 rows in st st, beg with a P row.
◊ Rep last 4 rows once more. (10 sts)
◊ Next row: K2tog, K6, ssk. (8 sts)
◊ Next row: P2tog, P4, p2tog. (6 sts)
◊ Cast off pwise.

Front legs

Make 2
◊ Using size 3 mm (US 2/3) needles, cast on 6 sts in black.
◊ Work 6 rows in st st, beg with a K row.
◊ Break black yarn and join rust yarn.
◊ Work 10 rows in st st, beg with a K row.
◊ Cast off.

Tail

Make 1
◊ Using size 3 mm (US 2/3) needles, cast on 4 sts in rust.
◊ Work 4 rows in st st, beg with a K row.
◊ Next row: K1, M1, K to last st, M1, K1. (6 sts)
◊ Work 3 rows in st st, beg with a P row.
◊ Rep last 4 rows once more. (8 sts)
◊ Next row: K1, k2tog, K2, ssk, K1. (6 sts)
◊ Next row: P.

◊ Break rust yarn and join a triple strand of white mohair yarn.
◊ Work 4 rows in st st, beg with a K row.
◊ Next row: K2tog, K2, ssk. (4 sts)
◊ Next row: P.
◊ Next row: K2tog, ssk. (2 sts)
◊ Next row: P2tog. (1 st)
◊ Break yarn and pull through rem st.

Ears

Make 4 pieces
◊ Using size 2.75 mm (US 2) needles, cast on 4 sts in rust.
◊ Work 4 rows in st st, beg with a K row.
◊ Next row: K2tog, ssk. (2 sts)
◊ Next row: P2tog. (1 st)
◊ Next row: Inc1. (2 sts)
◊ Next row: [Inc1 pwise] twice. (4 sts)
◊ Work 4 rows in st st, beg with a K row.
◊ Cast off.

Making up

Fold the head piece RS together and oversew the back seam, leaving the top open for turning and stuffing. Turn the head RS out and stuff. Make sure that the back seam is in the centre and close the top of the head using mattress stitch.

Fold the body piece in half lengthways, WS together. Seam the lower and back edges using mattress stitch, leaving the neck edge open for stuffing. Stuff the body. Oversew the head to the body. Oversew the belly to the underside of the head and body piece, so that the cast-off edge is stitched just under the chin and the cast-on edge is between the back legs.

Place two ear pieces WS together. Repeat for the second ear. Oversew at the sides, then oversew the ears in place.

Fold the tail in half lengthways, WS together. Oversew the seam, stuffing the tail lightly as you go. Stitch in place.

Fold the front leg pieces lengthways, WS together. Oversew the short edges and join the long seams using mattress stitch, leaving the top edge open for stuffing. Stuff and stitch in place.

Fold the back leg pieces lengthways, RS together. Oversew the seam on the top part of the legs, leaving the top edge open for stuffing. Turn RS out and sew the lower part of the seam using mattress stitch. Oversew the short edges. Stuff and oversew in place.

Work a small circle of chain stitch for the nose, using black yarn. Using a double strand of white mohair yarn, work two circles of small chain stitches around the nose. For the eyes, work two French knots using black yarn. Using white yarn, work a circle of chain stitch around each French knot.

To give your fox a fuzzy look, dampen him slightly and brush with a small nylon bristle brush.

Good night! Sleep well!

The moon has risen, supper has been eaten, and both farmers are taking a well-earned rest with a cup of cocoa before bed. After a long day in the fresh air, everyone's feeling sleepy. Bess and Max are in their regular places near to the stove, and it's almost bedtime. After all, it'll be another early start tomorrow. Good night!

Index